Sanjeev Kapoor's

SUNDAY SPECIALS

In association with Alyona Kapoor

Popular Prakashan
www.popularprakashan.com

Published by
POPULAR PRAKASHAN PVT. LTD.
301, Mahalaxmi Chambers
22, Bhulabhai Desai Road
Mumbai - 400 026
for KHANA KHAZANA PUBLICATIONS PVT. LTD.

First Published 2009
Fourth Reprint 2014

(4327)
ISBN: 978-81-7991-579-0

Design: Anjali Sawant
Typesetting: Satyavan Rane

PRINTED IN INDIA
by Saurabh Printers Pvt. Ltd.
A-16, Sector 4, Noida

AUTHOR'S NOTE

Sunday is the one day in the week that everybody looks forward to - it spells out fun, relaxation and best of all - Sunday Lunch! Here are some ideas for home-cooked meals that you can enjoy in the company of family and friends.

If a lazy Sunday is your idea of bliss, there are *biryanis* that will leave you with a delicious feeling of langour that can only be cured by a Sunday nap; mutton delights, rice drenched in hearty chicken and prawn curries, pastas covered in a blanket of cheese sauce, and thick filling *paranthe*, all guarantee to put you into a well-earned state of Sunday stupor.

But if for you, Sundays are fun days, full of vim and vigour, opt for energy-giving dishes like Chickpea and Tahina Salad or Burritos with a peppy Salsa Fresca, that will power you through the holiday. A selection of quick, hearty snacks and sweet temptations are also on offer to make your Sundays truly special!

Happy Sundays!

CONTENTS

SALADS

SNACKS

MAIN COURSE

SWEETS

Chickpea And Tahina Salad

Ingredients

2 cups boiled chickpeas

½ tablespoon tahina (sesame seed paste)

½ cup Mayonnaise (see alongside)

1 tablespoon olive oil

2 teaspoons lemon juice

Salt to taste

Black pepper powder to taste

1 medium cucumber, seeded and diced

1 medium tomato, seeded and diced

1 medium carrot, coarsely grated

Method

1. Place the tahina and mayonnaise in a small bowl. Whisk in the olive oil and lemon juice with a wire whisk. Add the salt and pepper powder to taste. Place the chickpeas, cucumber, tomato and carrot in a large bowl.
2. Pour the dressing over the chickpeas and toss to mix. Serve immediately with sliced wholewheat or pita bread.

Mayonnaise

Place 1 egg yolk, salt to taste, ¼ teaspoon each white pepper powder, French mustard and sugar and 1 teaspoon vinegar in a clean bowl and mix thoroughly with a whisk. Alternatively, process the mixture in a blender. Add 1 cup of oil, a little at a time, whisking or blending continuously, until all the oil is incorporated. Add 1 teaspoon lemon juice and adjust seasoning. Store in an airtight jar in a refrigerator.

Paneer And Pineapple Salad

Ingredients

300 grams cottage cheese, cut into ½-inch cubes

½ small fresh pineapple, cut into cubes

1 large unpeeled cucumber, cut into 1-inch pieces

1 medium green capsicum, cut into 1-inch pieces

½ small head of iceberg lettuce, roughly torn

6-8 black olives, stoned and sliced

1 teaspoon garlic paste

1 tablespoon lemon juice

1 teaspoon red chilli powder

½ teaspoon mixed dried herbs

Salt to taste

1½ tablespoons oil

Dressing

3 tablespoons salad oil

4 tablespoons vinegar

1 teaspoon sugar

1 teaspoon mustard powder

5-6 black peppercorns, crushed

½ teaspoon white pepper powder

Method

1. Combine the garlic paste, lemon juice, chilli powder, dried herbs and salt. Rub the mixture into the cottage cheese cubes and set aside to marinate, preferably in a refrigerator, for fifteen to twenty minutes.

2. Mix together all the ingredients for the dressing in a bowl.

3. Thread the cottage cheese cubes onto the skewers. Heat the oil on a *tawa* and place the skewers on it. Cook, turning the skewers a few times, to brown the cottage cheese evenly on all sides. Take the cottage cheese cubes off the skewers and place them on a plate and set aside to cool.

4. Combine the grilled cottage cheese, the pineapple, cucumber, capsicum, roughly torn lettuce and the olives in a large serving bowl. Drizzle the dressing over the salad and toss to mix well. Serve immediately.

Tropical Chicken And Farfalle Salad

Ingredients

200 grams boneless chicken, boiled and shredded

1 cup farfalle (bow-tie pasta)

1 medium tomato, cut into ½-inch cubes

1 medium carrot, cut into ½-inch cubes

½ medium green capsicum, cut into ½-inch cubes

½ medium yellow capsicum, cut into ½-inch cubes (optional)

8-10 olives, sliced into rings

Dressing

4-5 garlic cloves, chopped

2 inch celery stalk, finely chopped

½ teaspoon crushed fresh red chillies

2-3 tablespoons lemon juice

Salt to taste

2 teaspoons finely chopped fresh parsley

Method

1. Boil three cups of water in a deep pan. Add the pasta and cook till just done (al dente). Drain and set aside to cool.

2. To make the dressing, combine the garlic, celery, red chillies, lemon juice, salt and parsley in a bowl.

3. In a separate bowl, combine the pasta, chicken, tomato, carrot, green and yellow capsicums and olives.

4. Pour the dressing over and toss to mix. Serve immediately.

— Chef's Tip —

Pasta is cooked to perfection when it is 'al dente' - cooked but still firm to the bite.

Masala Sandwich Double Roti Chaat

Ingredients

8 *pav*

4 medium potatoes, boiled and mashed

2 teaspoons oil

½ teaspoon mustard seeds

1 teaspoon red chilli powder

¼ teaspoon turmeric powder

½ teaspoon *garam masala* powder

Salt to taste

3-4 tablespoons butter

4 tablespoons Green Chutney (see below)

4 tablespoons Date and Tamarind Chutney (see below)

1 medium onion, chopped

8 tablespoons *sev*

4 tablespoons chopped fresh coriander

Method

1. Heat the oil in a pan; add the mustard seeds. When they begin to splutter, add the mashed potatoes, chilli powder, turmeric powder, *garam masala* powder and salt.

2. Mix well and cook for three or four minutes. Remove and set aside. Slit two *pav* horizontally, but do not cut through to separate the halves.

3. Spread some butter on the insides of the *pav*. Stuff with the potato mixture and lightly toast the *pav* on a *tawa* using a little butter.

4. Arrange two roasted *pav* on each serving plate. Top with green chutney, date and tamarind chutney, onion and a generous helping of *sev*.

5. Garnish with chopped coriander and serve immediately.

Green Chutney

Grind together 1 cup fresh coriander, ½ cup fresh mint, 2-3 green chillies, black salt to taste, ¼ teaspoon sugar and 1 tablespoon lemon juice to a smooth paste using a little water if required.

Date and Tamarind Chutney

Wash, stone and chop 15-20 dates. Dry-roast 2 teaspoons cumin seeds and ¼ teaspoon fennel seeds. Cool and grind to a powder. Cook dates, 1 cup tamarind pulp, cumin and fennel powder, ½ cup jaggery, 2 teaspoons red chilli powder, 1 teaspoon dried ginger powder, black salt, salt and four cups of water till thick.

Burritos with Salsa Fresca

Ingredients

4 refined flour tortillas

1 ½ cups refried beans

6 lettuce leaves, roughly torn

2 medium onions, peeled and finely chopped

1 cup grated cheese

1 cup Salsa Fresca (see below)

Method

1. Mix together the beans, lettuce, onions and cheese.
2. Heat the tortillas on a *tawa* until hot and pliable, making sure they do not dry out.
3. Place two tablespoons of the bean mixture a little below the centre of each tortilla.
4. Add the salsa fresca and fold in the sides of the tortilla towards the centre.
5. Fold the bottom over the filling and roll up, enclosing the filling completely.
6. Serve immediately as burritos tend to become soggy.

Salsa Fresca

Ingredients

4 medium tomatoes

1 medium onion, peeled and very finely chopped

2 jalapeño chillies, finely chopped

2 teaspoons olive oil

1 teaspoon vinegar

Juice of ½ lemon

½ teaspoon salt

½ teaspoon dried oregano

¼ cup fresh coriander

Method

1. Score the bottom end of the tomatoes and immerse in boiling water for half a minute. Peel, remove seeds and chop roughly.
2. Combine the tomatoes, onion and jalapeño chillies in a bowl.
3. Add the olive oil, vinegar, lemon juice and salt. Crush the oregano and add to the sauce.
4. Mix well and leave to stand for at least two hours for the flavours to blend. Stir in the roughly chopped coriander. Serve at room temperature with snacks or as a dip.

— Chef's Tip —

Red wine vinegar is recommended, but you can substitute it with regular vinegar.

Potato Pizza

Ingredients

6-7 medium potatoes, boiled

2-3 garlic cloves

½ cup warm milk

Salt to taste

3 tablespoons olive oil

Topping

2 tablespoons olive oil

3-4 garlic cloves, crushed

1 cup Tomato Concasse (page 42)

½ cup tomato ketchup

3-4 fresh basil leaves, roughly torn

8-10 green olives, stoned and sliced

1 cup grated mozzarella cheese

2 jalapeño chillies, sliced

1 medium green capsicum, chopped

Salt to taste

10-12 black peppercorns, crushed

Method

1. Mash the boiled potatoes together with the garlic, milk, salt and one tablespoon of olive oil. Pass the

mixture through a soup strainer (*puran yantra*). Divide into two portions.

2. For the topping, heat the olive oil in a pan; add the garlic and sauté for half a minute. Add the tomato concasse and cook for another three to four minutes. Stir in the tomato ketchup and adjust seasonings. Set aside to cool.

3. Preheat the oven to 200°C/400°F/ Gas Mark 6.

4. Spread one part of the potato mixture evenly over the base of a large pizza pan.

5. Pour the cooled tomato mixture over the potato base and top with basil, olives, mozzarella cheese, jalapeño chillies, capsicum, salt and crushed peppercorns.

6. Cover with the remaining potato mixture and brush the top with the remaining olive oil.

7. Place the pan in the oven and bake for twenty to twenty-five minutes or till the top turns golden brown.

8. Remove from the oven, cut into wedges and serve immediately.

Smoky Paneer Wrap

Ingredients

300 grams cottage cheese, cut into thin strips

4 wholewheat *roomali roti*

2 tablespoons vinegar

2 green chillies, sliced

2 tablespoons oil

½ teaspoon garlic paste

½ teaspoon ginger paste

1 small onion, sliced

1 medium green capsicum, cut into strips

1 teaspoon red chilli powder

¼ teaspoon turmeric powder

1 teaspoon dried mango powder

Salt to taste

½ cup bean sprouts

1 tablespoon ghee

4 large lettuce leaves

Method

1. Combine the vinegar and green chillies in a bowl.

2. Heat the oil in a pan; add the garlic paste and ginger paste and sauté

for half a minute. Add the onion and continue to sauté for half a minute longer.

3. Add the capsicum, chilli powder, turmeric powder, dried mango powder, salt and cottage cheese and sauté over medium heat for two minutes.

4. Add the bean sprouts and continue to sauté for another minute. Remove from heat and set aside.

5. To obtain a smoky flavour, place a live charcoal in a bowl and place the bowl in the centre of the cottage cheese mixture. Pour a tablespoon of hot ghee over the charcoal, cover immediately and leave for three to four minutes. Remove the bowl from the cottage cheese mixture.

6. To make the wraps, divide the cottage cheese mixture into four equal portions. Place a lettuce leaf on a *roomali roti*. Spread a portion of cottage cheese mixture over the *roti* and drizzle with half a teaspoon of chilli-vinegar.

7. Roll up, wrap in aluminium foil and serve immediately.

Parotta Kurma

Ingredients

4-5 medium boiled potatoes, cut into 1-inch cubes

4 dried red chillies

1 tablespoon coriander seeds

½ tablespoon cumin seeds

1 inch ginger, roughly chopped

4-5 garlic cloves

3 tablespoons oil

½ teaspoon turmeric powder

1 teaspoon *garam masala* powder

½ cup yogurt, whisked

Salt to taste

2 tablespoons chopped fresh coriander

Parotta

1½ cups wholewheat flour

Salt to taste

½ cup pure ghee

1 tablespoon yogurt

Method

1. To make the *kurma*, dry-roast the red chillies, coriander seeds and cumin seeds; grind to a paste along with the ginger, garlic and some water to a fine paste.
2. Heat the oil in a *kadai;* add the ground paste and fry for two to three minutes till the oil separates.

3. Add the turmeric powder, *garam masala* powder, yogurt and salt. Stir and cook, covered, over low heat for one minute.

4. Stir in the potatoes and chopped coriander and continue to cook over low heat for two to three minutes, or till the oil separates. Remove from heat and keep warm.

5. To make the *parottas*, reserve a little flour for dusting, and sift the rest together with salt.

6. Add three tablespoons of ghee and yogurt and knead with some water into a soft dough.

7. Divide the dough into eight equal portions and roll into balls.

8. Roll out each ball on a lightly floured surface. Spread half a tablespoon of melted ghee over the *roti*, fold twice to make a triangle. Roll out again to make a medium thick *parotta*.

9. Heat a *tawa* and fry the *parotta* on both sides. Drizzle some ghee around the *parotta* and shallow-fry till both sides are crisp and brown. Serve hot with *aloo kurma*.

Naan Sandwich

Ingredients

4 *naan* (see note below)

2 tablespoons oil + for shallow-frying

2 large onions, chopped

2 medium tomatoes, chopped

Salt to taste

2-3 green chillies, chopped

2 teaspoons red chilli powder

¼ teaspoon turmeric powder

3 eggs

2 large boiled potatoes, grated or finely chopped

2 tablespoons chopped fresh coriander

Method

1. Heat two tablespoons of oil in a non-stick pan; add the onions and sauté over medium heat till light golden.

2. Add the tomatoes and salt and continue to cook for another two minutes.

3. Add the green chillies, chilli powder and turmeric powder. Stir and cook for two minutes, or till the oil separates.

4. Add the eggs and cook for one minute without stirring. When set, stir lightly with a wooden spatula and cook till done.

5. Add the potatoes and chopped coriander. Mix well and remove from heat.

6. To prepare each sandwich, split a *naan* in half to make two flat rounds. Place a generous portion of the potato and egg filling on one half, spread evenly and then place the other half of the naan on top and press lightly.

7. Heat a teaspoon of oil on a non-stick *tawa*; place the *naan* sandwich and cook over low heat for one minute. Carefully flip the *naan* over, drizzle some more oil around and cook for another minute.

8. Remove from the *tawa* carefully and cut into quarters and serve with Green Chutney (page 14) and onion rings.

— Chef's Tip —

Instead of eggs, you can use a spicy cooked chicken or mutton keema and then add the potatoes.

Note: The naan used in this recipe are not the same as the familiar *tandoori naans*. They are more like Indian pizza bread and can be bought from Muslim bakeries or in Muslim localities.

Chicken Kathi Rolls

Ingredients

4-6 refined flour *roti*

300 grams boneless chicken, cubed

½ tablespoon ginger paste

½ tablespoon garlic paste

Salt to taste

2 tablespoons oil

½ teaspoon roasted cumin powder

½ teaspoon coriander powder

½ teaspoon red chilli powder

¼ teaspoon *chaat masala*

2 medium onions, sliced

1 medium carrot, cut into strips

4-6 tablespoons Green Chutney (page 14)

2 tablespoons chopped fresh coriander

Method

1. Mix together the ginger paste, garlic paste and salt and marinate the chicken cubes in the mixture for one hour, preferably in the refrigerator.

2. Heat the oil in a pan and sauté the chicken cubes till tender. Add the roasted cumin powder, coriander powder, chilli powder, *chaat masala* and salt. Keep warm.

3. In a bowl, mix together the sliced onions and carrot strips.

4. To make each *kathi* roll, put one teaspoon of oil on a *tawa* and lightly heat the *roti*.

5. Spread one teaspoon of green chutney over the *roti*, place six to eight pieces of cooked chicken on top and sprinkle with the chopped coriander.

6. Spread a spoonful of onion and carrot mixture on top and sprinkle salt. Roll the *roti* up tightly and serve.

Note: For a vegetarian version, replace the chicken with cottage cheese or boiled potato cubes.

Vegetable Ishtew And Appam

Ingredients

2 medium carrots, cubed

2 medium potatoes, cubed

7-8 cauliflower florets

6–8 French beans, cut into 1-inch pieces

2 tablespoons coconut oil

2 bay leaves

2 one-inch cinnamon sticks

4 cloves

2 star anise

10–12 curry leaves

4 green chillies, slit

2 medium onions, chopped

2 teaspoons ginger-garlic paste

1 cup thin Coconut Milk (see below)

Salt to taste

1 cup thick Coconut Milk (see below)

A pinch of *garam masala* powder

Method

1. Parboil the carrots, potatoes, cauliflower florets and French beans separately. Drain and set aside.

2. Heat the coconut oil in a deep pan. Add the bay leaves, cinnamon, cloves, star anise, curry leaves, green chillies and onions, and sauté for two minutes.

3. Add the ginger-garlic paste, stir and cook for a minute.

4. Add the carrots, potatoes and cauliflower and the thin coconut milk and cook for two to three minutes. Add salt and the French beans and cook till the French beans are tender.

5. Stir in the thick coconut milk and the *garam masala* powder. Remove from heat immediately and serve hot with Appam (see next page).

Coconut Milk

Process 1 cup grated fresh coconut in a blender with ¼ cup warm water. Pass the ground coconut through a muslin cloth or strainer pressing firmly to extract all the juice, or first milk. Add a quarter cup of warm water to the strained coconut to get the second, thinner milk from the same solids.

Appam

Ingredients

1 cup rice

1 cup parboiled rice

¼ cup coconut water

Salt to taste

¾ cup grated coconut

¼ teaspoon baking powder

Oil to grease the *appam tawa*

Method

1. Soak both the varieties of rice together in four cups of water for two to three hours. Drain and grind to a smooth paste adding the coconut water, as required.

2. Add the salt, stir well and set aside in a warm place to ferment for at least thirty-six hours.

3. Soak the grated coconut in one and a half cups of warm water; grind and extract thick milk. Add the coconut milk to the fermented batter to dilute it to a thick and creamy consistency. Mix in the baking powder and adjust the salt.

4. Heat an *appam tawa*; brush it with a little oil. Pour in one ladleful of batter and tilt the *tawa* all round to spread the batter. The edges should be thin and the excess batter should collect in the centre at the bottom.

5. Cover with a thick heavy lid and cook over medium heat for two to thee minutes. Check to see if the sides start leaving the *tawa*. The edges of the *appam* should be crisp and thin and the centre soft and spongy.

6. Serve hot with Vegetable Ishtew (page 32).

— Chef's Tip —

- Traditionally fresh toddy is used to ferment *appam* batter. In the above recipe, the coconut water acts as the fermenting agent.

- A special cast iron *appam tawa* is used to make *appams*. However, you may use a small non-stick *kadai*.

Vegetable Massaman Curry

Ingredients

6-8 broccoli florets

1 medium red capsicum , cut into 1-inch pieces

1 medium green capsicum, cut into 1-inch pieces

1 medium yellow capsicum, cut into 1-inch pieces

3 tablespoons Massaman Curry Paste (recipe below)

1 tablespoon oil

1 tablespoon soy sauce

1 tablespoon lemon juice

2 tablespoons roasted peanuts

Salt to taste

Method

1. Heat the oil in a pan; add the vegetables and sauté for five to six minutes.
2. Stir in the soy sauce, lemon juice and roasted peanuts.
3. Add the curry paste and salt to taste and mix well.
4. Cook for another fifteen minutes and serve hot.

Massaman Curry Paste

Ingredients

4 spring onions, finely chopped

12 garlic cloves, chopped

1 inch galangal

1 lemon grass stalk, chopped

2 cloves

1 tablespoon coriander seeds

1 teaspoon cumin seeds

5 black peppercorns

3 dried red chillies, soaked and chopped

1 teaspoon salt

1 teaspoon shrimp paste (optional)

Method

1. Cook the spring onions, garlic, galangal, lemon grass, cloves, coriander seeds and cumin seeds in a wok over low heat for about five minutes. Grind to a paste.
2. Add the peppercorns, red chillies and salt and grind again.
3. Add the shrimp paste and grind again.

Makes half a cup of curry paste.

Baked Mixed Vegetables

Ingredients

3 medium brinjals, sliced

4 medium potatoes, boiled and sliced

1 medium green capsicum, sliced

1 medium red capsicum, sliced

Salt to taste

2 tablespoons oil

2 medium onions, cut into round slices, rings separated

¼ cup Vegetable Stock (see below)

10-12 black peppercorns, crushed

½ cup fresh breadcrumbs

½ cup grated processed cheese

Tomato Sauce

1 cup tomato concasse (see below)

2 tablespoons oil

3-4 garlic cloves, chopped

4-5 black peppercorns

1 bay leaf

Salt to taste

Cheese Sauce

¼ cup grated processed cheese

½ cup White Sauce (see below)

Method

1. Preheat an oven to 200°C/400°F/ Gas Mark 6.

2. Sprinkle salt on the brinjal slices. Place in a colander for thirty minutes to drain. Rinse under cold running water and pat dry with paper towels.

3. Arrange the brinjal slices on a baking tray and grill in the preheated oven till golden brown.

4. Heat the oil in a pan. Add the onion rings and sauté for a minute. Add the green and red capsicums and sauté for one or two minutes. Set aside.

5. For the tomato sauce, heat the oil in a pan. Add the garlic and sauté for one minute. Add the tomato concasse and sauté for two or three minutes. Add the peppercorns, bay leaf and salt and continue to cook for two or three minutes, or till the sauce thickens.

6. To make the cheese sauce, add the grated cheese to the white sauce and mix well.

7. Add the cheese sauce to the tomato sauce; add the vegetable stock and bring the mixture to a boil. Remove from heat and strain.

8. In a seven-inch square baking dish, layer the onions, green and red capsicums followed by the brinjals and potatoes. Sprinkle salt and crushed peppercorns over each layer. Pour the tomato-cheese sauce over all the vegetables.
9. Sprinkle the fresh breadcrumbs and top with the grated cheese. Bake for about twenty minutes, or till the cheese turns golden. Serve hot with brown bread.

Tomato Concasse

To make 1 cup of tomato concasse , blanch 5 medium tomatoes in plenty of boiling water for two minutes. Drain and refresh in cold water; peel, cut in half, remove the seeds and chop roughly.

Vegetable Stock

Place 1 sliced onion, 1 sliced carrot, one 2-3 inch celery stalk, 2 garlic cloves, 1 bay leaf, 5-6 black peppercorns and 2-3 cloves in a pan with five cups of water and bring to a boil. Simmer for 15 minutes and strain

White Sauce

Ingredients

1 ½ tablespoons refined flour

2 tablespoons butter

1 medium onion

1 bay leaf

2 cloves

1 ½ cups milk

A small pinch of grated nutmeg

Salt to taste

¼ teaspoon white pepper powder

Method

1. Melt one and a half tablespoons of butter in a thick-bottomed pan. Add the flour; stir and cook the roux (butter-flour mixture) over low heat with a wooden spoon. When it develops a sandy texture, remove from heat and cool.
2. Peel the onion. Wrap a bay leaf around it studding it with cloves at the two ends. Bring the milk to a boil with the onion. Remove onion.
3. Pour the boiling hot milk into the cold roux, stirring continuously, to prevent lumps from forming.
4. Simmer gently for two minutes. Add nutmeg and seasoning. Melt the remaining butter and gently pour over the top of the sauce to prevent a skin forming.

Oodles Of Noodles

Ingredients

200 grams noodles

1 tablespoon oil

2 spring onions, sliced

1 small yellow capsicum, sliced

1 small red capsicum, sliced

4-5 French beans, sliced diagonally and blanched

½ cup sweetcorn kernels, boiled

2 teaspoons soy sauce

Salt to taste

2 tablespoons hot and sweet tomato ketchup

1 tablespoon sweet chilli sauce

¼ cup bean sprouts

2 stalks spring onion greens, sliced

Method

1. Boil the noodles in plenty of salted water. Drain, refresh in cold water and set aside.

2. Heat the oil in a pan; add the spring onions and stir-fry for a while.

3. Add the capsicums and French beans and stir-fry for a few minutes.

4. Add the sweetcorn and soy sauce and mix well. Add the noodles and salt and toss to mix.
5. Add the hot and sweet tomato ketchup and sweet chilli sauce and mix gently.
6. Add the bean sprouts and spring onion greens and mix well.
7. Serve hot.

Cheesy Macaroni

Ingredients

1 cup grated processed cheese

300 grams macaroni, boiled

6 tablespoons butter

2 tablespoons refined flour

2 cups milk

Salt to taste

White pepper powder to taste

2 tablespoons fresh breadcrumbs

½ teaspoon crushed black peppercorns

½ tablespoon chopped fresh parsley

Method

1. Preheat the oven to 220°C/425°F/ Gas Mark 7.
2. Heat two tablespoons of butter in a pan; add the flour and sauté lightly, making sure that it does not change colour.
3. Gradually add the milk, stirring continuously, so that no lumps form.
4. Add half the grated cheese and continue to stir. After adding the cheese, the sauce will thicken further, so add more milk to adjust the consistency. Add salt and white pepper powder and mix well.
5. Heat two tablespoons of butter in a separate pan. Add the macaroni and toss to mix. Strain the sauce into the pan and mix gently.
6. Add the remaining cheese and transfer the mixture into a seven-inch square baking dish.
7. Sprinkle the breadcrumbs over the top and dot with the remaining butter. Sprinkle the crushed peppercorns and parsley. Bake till the cheese melts and turns golden. Serve hot.

Dal Dhokli

Ingredients

¾ cup split pigeon peas

¾ cup wholewheat flour

2 tablespoons gram flour

Salt to taste

¾ teaspoon turmeric powder

¾ teaspoon red chilli powder

2 pinches asafoetida

½ tablespoon oil

1½ tablespoons peanuts

1 tablespoon ghee

¼ teaspoon mustard seeds

½ teaspoon cumin seeds

4 garlic cloves, peeled and finely chopped

4 curry leaves

3 rinds of gamboge

1½ teaspoons grated jaggery

2 tablespoons chopped fresh coriander

Method

1. Soak the pigeon peas in two cups of water for half an hour.

2. Mix together the wholewheat flour and gram flour. Add salt, one-fourth teaspoon turmeric powder, chilli powder, a pinch of asafoetida, oil and enough water to make a stiff dough. Roll the dough out into thin rotis and cut into desired shapes (*dhokli*).

3. Boil the split pigeon peas with one and a half cups of water. When the split pigeon peas is half-cooked, add the peanuts and remaining turmeric powder.

4. Heat the ghee in a pan; add the mustard seeds, cumin seeds, remaining asafoetida, garlic and curry leaves, and sauté for a few seconds. Pour the sizzling spices into the *dal*. Add two cups of water and the gamboge and bring to a boil; stir in the jaggery.

5. Add the strips of dough and cook, stirring occasionally, so that the *dhokli* do not stick to the bottom of the pan.

6. Adjust salt and serve hot, garnished with chopped coriander.

Chilli-Mushroom Fried Rice

Ingredients

4 green chillies, finely chopped

1 ½ cups sliced fresh button mushrooms

1 ½ cups cooked rice

3 tablespoons oil

1 inch ginger, finely chopped

6-8 garlic cloves, chopped

5-6 spring onions, finely chopped

A pinch of MSG (optional)

½ teaspoon white pepper powder

Salt to taste

1 tablespoon soy sauce

3-4 spring onion greens, finely chopped

Method

1. Heat the oil in a wok; add the ginger, garlic and green chillies and stir-fry for two minutes.
2. Add the spring onions, mushrooms, MSG, white pepper powder and salt, and stir-fry over high heat for two minutes.
3. Add the rice, soy sauce and spring onion greens. Stir-fry over high heat for three minutes.
4. Serve hot.

Ek Handi Nu Dal Bhaat

Ingredients

½ cup split pigeon peas

¾ cup rice

3 tablespoons ghee

½ teaspoon cumin seeds

2-3 cloves

4-5 black peppercorns

1 bay leaf

1 medium onion, sliced

¾ teaspoon ginger paste

¾ teaspoon garlic paste

1 large potato, peeled and cut into 1-inch pieces

¼ teaspoon turmeric powder

¾ teaspoon red chilli powder

¼ teaspoon *garam masala* powder

2 green chillies, chopped

Salt to taste

1 large tomato, puréed

2 tablespoons chopped fresh coriander

Method

1. Heat the ghee in a pan; add the cumin seeds, cloves, peppercorns and bay leaf and sauté till fragrant. Add the onion, ginger paste and garlic paste and sauté for one more minute.
2. Add the potato and mix well. Stir in the pigeon peas and rice.
3. Add the turmeric powder, chilli powder, *garam masala* powder and green chillies and mix well. Add four cups of water and salt.
4. Bring to a boil, lower heat, cover and cook till almost done. Stir in the tomato purée and chopped coriander. Mash the mixture slightly with the back of a ladle.
5. Cook, covered, over low heat for eight to ten minutes and serve.

Tiranga Kofta Pulao

Ingredients

1 ½ cups Basmati rice, soaked
3 tablespoons ghee
3 small onions, sliced
Salt to taste

Cottage Cheese Kofta

150 grams cottage cheese, grated
Salt to taste
¼ teaspoon white pepper powder
½ teaspoon green cardamom powder
1 ½ tablespoons cornflour
Oil for deep-frying

Green Rice

1 medium bunch (200 grams) spinach
1 green chilli
2 garlic cloves

White Rice

1 teaspoon cumin seeds

Yellow Rice

A few saffron threads

Method

1. Mix the cottage cheese with the salt, white pepper powder and cardamom powder and mash well. Divide into eighteen equal portions and shape into balls. Dust with cornflour.
2. Heat sufficient oil in a *kadai* and deep-fry the cottage cheese balls till golden. Drain on absorbent paper.
3. Boil the rice with four cups of water till almost done; drain. Divide into three equal parts.

4. For the green rice, blanch the spinach in plenty of water. Drain and purée in a blender along with the green chilli and garlic.
5. Heat one tablespoon of ghee in a pan; add one-third of the onions and sauté till translucent. Add the spinach purée and sauté for one minute over high heat. Add one part of the rice along with six cottage cheese balls and salt and toss to mix. Transfer to a bowl and set aside.
6. For the white rice, heat one tablespoon of ghee in a pan; add the cumin seeds and when they begin to change colour, add half the remaining onions and sauté till translucent. Add another part of rice, six cottage cheese balls and salt and toss well. Transfer to a separate bowl and set aside.
7. For the yellow rice, soak the saffron in two tablespoons of water. Heat one tablespoon of ghee in a pan, add the remaining onions and sauté till translucent. Add the remaining rice with the saffron water. Add the cottage cheese balls and salt and toss to mix. Transfer to a bowl and set aside.
8. In a transparent square glass dish, spread a layer of green rice and level the surface. Spread a layer of white rice over the green rice and level the surface. Top with a layer of yellow rice. Alternatively, arrange the rice in a pattern on a flat dish.

Kolhapuri Chicken

Ingredients

1 whole (1 kg) chicken, cut into 12 pieces

5 tablespoons oil

3-4 dried red chillies

3 medium onions, chopped

2 teaspoons ginger paste

2 teaspoons garlic paste

¼ teaspoon turmeric powder

A pinch of grated nutmeg

1 teaspoon Kolhapuri dry chutney

Salt to taste

2 tablespoons chopped fresh coriander

Masala Paste

1 tablespoon sesame

2 tablespoons poppy seeds

6-8 black peppercorns

1 teaspoon caraway seeds

1 tablespoon cumin seeds

1 inch cinnamon

3-4 green cardamoms

1 black cardamom

4-5 cloves

1 blade of mace

¼ dried coconut, grated

8-10 Bedgi red chillies

Method

1. For the *masala* paste, dry-roast the sesame seeds, poppy seeds, peppercorns, caraway seeds, cumin seeds, cinnamon, green cardamoms, black cardamom, cloves, mace, dried coconut and Bedgi chillies separately. Cool and grind with a little water to a fine paste.
2. Heat the oil in a pressure cooker; add the red chillies, sauté for a few seconds, remove from heat and reserve for garnishing. Add the onions to the same oil and sauté till golden brown.
3. Add the ginger paste and garlic paste and cook over medium heat for a few seconds. Stir in the ground paste and cook for three or four minutes over medium heat, stirring frequently.
4. Add the chicken, mix well and cook over high heat, stirring continuously, for two or three minutes.
5. Add half a cup of water and continue cooking over medium heat for three or four minutes, stirring frequently.
6. Add the turmeric powder, grated nutmeg, Kolhapuri dry chutney and salt. Seal the cooker with the lid and cook till the pressure is released twice (two whistles).
7. Remove the lid when the pressure has reduced completely. The *masala* should be quite thick and dry.
8. Serve hot, garnished with chopped coriander and fried chillies.

Teewarn

Sindhi Mutton Chop Curry

Ingredients

1 kilogram mutton chops

6 tablespoons oil

1 teaspoon cumin seeds

2-3 cloves

2 green cardamoms

1 bay leaf

2 large onions, chopped

1 teaspoon ginger paste

½ tablespoon garlic paste

3 green chillies, chopped

3 medium tomatoes, chopped

Salt to taste

1 tablespoon red chilli powder

½ tablespoon coriander powder

¼ teaspoon turmeric powder

¼ cup yogurt

½ teaspoon *garam masala* powder

Method

1. Heat the oil in a pressure cooker; add the cumin seeds, cloves, cardamoms and bay leaf and sauté for half a minute.

2. When the spices begin to change colour, add the onions and sauté over medium heat till light golden.

3. Add the ginger paste, garlic paste, green chillies, tomatoes and salt and cook over low heat for two to three minutes.

4. Add the chilli powder, coriander powder, turmeric powder and mutton chops. Stir and continue to cook for three to four minutes.

5. Add the yogurt and one cup of water. Mix well. Pressure cook till the pressure is released six times (six whistles), or till the mutton is tender.

6. Remove the lid when the pressure reduces completely, stir in the *garam masala* powder and simmer for two minutes.

7. Serve hot with steamed rice.

Chicken And Spinach Bake

Ingredients

4 (200 grams each) boneless chicken breasts

2 bunches (500 grams) spinach, blanched and chopped

Salt to taste

1 teaspoon black pepper powder

½ teaspoon dried oregano

1 teaspoon vinegar

¼ teaspoon mustard paste

¼ teaspoon sugar

2 tablespoons oil

¼ cup raw rice, soaked

½ cup milk

½ cup grated processed cheese

1 small onion, chopped

¼ cup breadcrumbs

2 tablespoons butter

Method

1. Preheat the oven to 200°C/400°F/ Gas Mark 6.

2. Mix together the salt, pepper powder, oregano, vinegar, mustard paste and sugar. Rub the mixture all over the chicken and marinate for an hour preferably in a refrigerator.

3. Heat the oil in a pan and sauté the chicken breasts until both sides are golden brown.

4. Mix together the spinach, rice, milk, half the cheese, onion and salt in a large bowl. Spread the mixture at the bottom of a seven-inch square baking dish. Place the chicken on top of the spinach mixture.

5. Combine the breadcrumbs, butter and remaining cheese in a small bowl and sprinkle the mixture evenly over the chicken. Cover the dish with aluminium foil and bake for fifteen minutes.

6. Remove the foil and continue baking for five minutes, or until the spinach mixture has set and the chicken is no longer pink in the centre. Serve hot.

Shaan E Raan

Ingredients

1 whole (1 kg) leg of goat or lamb
4-5 tablespoons green unripe papaya paste
2 tablespoons garlic paste
2 tablespoons ginger paste
Salt to taste
½ cup oil
6 large onions, chopped
4 large tomatoes, chopped
½ teaspoon turmeric powder
2 tablespoons coriander powder
1 tablespoon roasted cumin powder
3-4 teaspoons red chilli powder
¼ teaspoon green cardamom powder
½ tablespoon *garam masala* powder
1 cup yogurt, whisked
2 tablespoons chopped fresh coriander
1 large onion, sliced into rings
A sprig of fresh mint

Method

1. Clean the leg of lamb and make small gashes all over. Combine the papaya paste, one and a half tablespoons of garlic paste, one and a half tablespoons of ginger paste and salt and rub the mixture all over

the lamb. Leave to marinate for two to three hours, preferably in a refrigerator.

2. Preheat the oven to 180°C/350°/Gas Mark 4.
3. Heat the oil in a pan; add the onions and sauté over medium heat till light golden. Add the remaining ginger paste and garlic paste and continue to sauté. Add the tomatoes and sauté for a few minutes.
4. Add the turmeric powder, coriander powder, roasted cumin powder and chilli powder to the *masala* in the pan and continue to sauté for a few minutes. Add the cardamom powder and *garam masala* powder and mix well. Stir in the yogurt, chopped coriander and salt.
5. Grease a baking tray and place the marinated leg of lamb in it.
6. Pour the *masala* over the leg of lamb. Cover with aluminium foil and cook in the oven for forty to forty-five minutes. Lower the temperature to 140°C/275°F/Gas Mark 1 and continue to bake for one hour.
7. Serve hot, garnished with onion rings and mint.

— Chef's Tip —

Marinate the leg of lamb overnight so that the meat cooks faster and will be tender.

Prawn Ghassi

Ingredients

18-20 (300 grams) medium prawns, peeled and deveined

Salt to taste

1 cup grated coconut

2 medium onions, peeled and chopped

4 dried red chillies, roasted

2 teaspoons coriander seeds

1 teaspoon cumin seeds

8-10 black peppercorns

¼ teaspoon fenugreek seeds

½ teaspoon turmeric powder

5 garlic cloves, peeled

1½ tablespoons Tamarind Pulp (see below)

3 tablespoons oil

Method

1. Wash the prawns thoroughly under running water. Drain and pat dry. Sprinkle with salt and set aside for one hour, preferably in the refrigerator.

2. Grind the grated coconut, half the chopped onions, the red chillies, coriander seeds, cumin seeds, peppercorns, fenugreek seeds, turmeric powder, garlic and tamarind pulp with enough water to a smooth paste.

3. Heat oil in a *kadai* and fry the remaining chopped onions till light brown.

4. Add the *masala* paste and sauté for two to three minutes. Add two cups of water and mix well. Bring the mixture to a boil; add the prawns and adjust seasoning. Simmer for five minutes.

5. Serve hot.

Tamarind Pulp

Soak 75 grams tamarind in 100 ml warm water for 10-15 minutes. Grind to a smooth paste and strain to remove any fibres. Store in an airtight container in the refrigerator.

Chicken Biryani

Ingredients

500 grams chicken on the bone, cut into 1½-inch pieces

1½ cups Sela rice, soaked

1 tablespoon ginger paste

1 tablespoon garlic paste

1 teaspoon green chilli paste

1 tablespoon coriander powder

1 tablespoon roasted cumin powder

1 teaspoon *garam masala* powder

1 teaspoon green cardamom powder

Salt to taste

1 cup yogurt

3 tablespoons oil

1 bay leaf

4 cloves

2 green cardamoms

1 black cardamom

5 cups Chicken Stock (page 79)

A few saffron threads

1 tablespoon milk

1 teaspoon caraway seeds

1 inch ginger, cut into thin strips

2 medium onions, sliced and deep-fried

½ cup chopped fresh mint

2 tablespoons chopped fresh coriander

1 teaspoon screw pine essence

1 teaspoon rose water

Method

1. Marinate the chicken in a mixture of ginger paste, garlic paste, green chilli paste, coriander powder, cumin powder, *garam masala* powder, cardamom powder, salt and yogurt for about half an hour.

2. Heat one tablespoon of oil in a pan. Add the bay leaf, cloves, green cardamoms and black cardamom and sauté for half a minute. Add the rice and sauté for a minute. Add the chicken stock and bring to a boil. Lower heat and cook for eight to ten minutes, or till the rice is three-fourth done. Drain and set aside. Soak the saffron in the milk.

3. Heat the remaining oil in a thick-bottomed pan. Add the caraway seeds and sauté till fragrant. Add the marinated chicken and sauté for three to four minutes or till half cooked.

4. Remove the pan from heat. Spread the rice over the chicken. Sprinkle the saffron-flavoured milk, ginger strips, fried onions, chopped mint and coriander, screw pine essence and rose water over the rice. Cover and cook on *dum* for fifteen to twenty minutes over low heat.

5. Serve hot with a *raita* of your choice.

Note: Sela rice is parboiled Basmati rice.

Kolambi Bhaat

Ingredients

2 cups Basmati rice, soaked

12-16 (150 grams) medium prawns, shelled and deveined

1 teaspoon lemon juice

Salt to taste

½ cup chopped fresh coriander

½ cup grated fresh coconut

3 green chillies, chopped

1 inch ginger, chopped

6-7 garlic cloves, chopped

12-15 fresh mint leaves

3 tablespoons oil

1 inch cinnamon

4 black cardamoms

2 star anise

4 cloves

1 teaspoon cumin seeds

2 medium onions, chopped

½ cup Coconut Milk (page 33)

Method

1. Marinate the prawns in lemon juice and salt.
2. Reserve one tablespoon each of chopped coriander and coconut for garnishing.
3. Grind the green chillies, ginger, garlic, remaining chopped coriander, mint leaves and remaining coconut to a fine paste.
4. Heat the oil in a thick-bottomed *handi*; add the cinnamon, black cardamoms, star anise, cloves and cumin seeds. Sauté for one minute.
5. Add the onions, sauté for three or four minutes or till light golden brown. Add the *masala* paste, sauté for half a minute and add the prawns. Sauté for two to three minutes.
6. Add the soaked rice and salt to taste and stir gently for one minute. Stir in the coconut milk.
7. Add two and a half cups of hot water and bring to a boil, stirring once or twice. Cook over medium heat till most of the water has been absorbed. Lower heat and cook, covered, till the rice is done.
8. Remove from heat and serve, garnished with the reserved chopped coriander and the grated coconut.

Jambalaya

Ingredients

1 ½ cups parboiled rice

4 tablespoons butter

1 medium onion, chopped

1 small green capsicum, cut into ½-inch pieces

1 small red capsicum, cut into ½-inch pieces

1 small yellow capsicum, cut into ½-inch pieces

¼ small broccoli, separated into florets

3 medium tomatoes, blanched and chopped

1 ½ teaspoons paprika

½ cup boneless chicken, cut into 1-inch cubes

2 chicken sausages, cut into ½-inch pieces

8-10 medium prawns, peeled and deveined

3 cups Chicken Stock (see below)

Salt to taste

Method

1. Soak the rice in three cups of water for half an hour. Drain.
2. Heat the butter in a pan; add the onion and sauté till translucent. Add the rice and stir-fry for one minute.
3. Add the capsicums, broccoli, tomatoes, paprika, chicken, chicken sausages and prawns. Sauté for one minute longer.
4. Add the chicken stock and salt and bring to a boil. Lower heat, cover and cook for twenty to thirty minutes, or till the rice is cooked. Serve hot.

Chicken Stock

Boil 200 grams chicken bones in water for 5 minutes. Drain and discard water.

Boil blanched bones with a roughly chopped carrot, celery stalk, leek, 2-3 parsley stalks, 6-7 black peppercorns, 5-6 cloves, 1 bay leaf and 10 cups of water.

Remove any scum which rises to the surface and replace it with more cold water. Simmer for at least one hour.

Remove from heat, strain, cool and store in a refrigerator till further use.

Keema Kulcha

Ingredients

1 ½ cups minced mutton

2 cups refined flour

Salt to taste

¼ teaspoon soda bicarbonate

2 tablespoons milk

2 tablespoons yogurt

3-4 garlic cloves, crushed

1 inch ginger, chopped

2 green chillies, chopped

1 medium onion, chopped

4 tablespoons chopped fresh coriander

Method

1. Sift the refined flour along with salt and the soda bicarbonate into a bowl. Add the milk and yogurt and mix. Add sufficient water and knead into a soft dough. Cover with a damp cloth and set aside for fifteen minutes. Divide the dough into eight equal portions.

2. Add the garlic, ginger, green chillies, onion, chopped coriander and salt to the minced mutton and mix well. Divide into eight equal portions.

3. Roll out each portion of the dough into a *puri*, place one portion of the mutton mixture in the centre, gather in the edges and roll into a ball. Roll out again as thin as possible. Heat a pressure cooker. Brush a little water

on one side of the *kulcha* and press it onto the inner wall of the cooker.

4. Similarly press two more *kulchas* onto the inner wall of the cooker. Invert the cooker over a gas flame and cook over a medium heat for two to three minutes.
5. Remove the *kulchas* with tongs and serve hot with Burnt Garlic and Mint Chutney (see below).

Burnt Garlic and Mint Chutney

Ingredients

20-25 garlic cloves

3 cups fresh mint, roughly torn

1 tablespoon oil

½ teaspoon black salt

1 inch ginger, roughly chopped

2 green chillies, roughly chopped

1½ cups yogurt, whisked

1 tablespoon lemon juice

Salt to taste

Method

1. Heat the oil in a pan; add the garlic and sauté. Sprinkle black salt and sauté till well browned. Grind together the mint, ginger, green chillies, sautéed garlic, two tablespoons of water to a fine paste.
2. Add the paste to the yogurt and mix well. Add the lemon juice and salt and mix again. Pass the mixture through a piece of muslin, squeezing well to get a smooth chutney. Serve chilled.

Mutton Dhansaak

Ingredients

450 grams boneless lean lamb or mutton, cubed

¼ cup split pigeon peas

¼ cup split red lentils

2 medium onions, sliced

1 inch ginger, chopped

5–6 garlic cloves, chopped

10 black peppercorns

2 green chillies, slit and seeded

½ teaspoon turmeric powder

1 teaspoon red chilli powder

100 grams pumpkin, cut into ½-inch cubes

3 medium brinjals, cut into ½-inch cubes

1 large potato, cut into ½-inch cubes

1 teaspoon salt

¼ medium bunch (75 grams) fresh fenugreek, chopped

10-15 fresh mint, chopped

2 medium tomatoes, chopped

2 tablespoons *dhansaak masala*

3 tablespoons Tamarind Pulp (page 71)

2 tablespoons chopped fresh coriander

Method

1. Soak the pigeon peas and red lentils in two cups water for thirty minutes. Drain. Heat a non-stick pan. Add the onions and roast over low heat for two to three minutes.

2. Add the ginger and garlic and stir for three to four minutes. Add the lamb and continue to cook for eight to ten minutes, until the meat is lightly browned on all sides.

3. Stir in the peppercorns, chillies, turmeric powder and chilli powder and mix. Add the soaked pigeon peas and red lentils and mix well.

4. Add the pumpkin, brinjals, potato, salt and three and a half cups of water. Bring to a boil and cook for ten minutes.

5. Stir in the fresh fenugreek and mint, followed by the tomatoes. Cover and cook over low heat until the mutton is cooked – this may take thirty to forty-five minutes. If you are using a pressure cooker, cook till the pressure is released six times (six whistles.)

6. Once the lamb is cooked, take off the heat and remove the meat from the mixture.

7. Stir the *dhansaak masala* and tamarind pulp into the *dal* mixture. Set aside to cool.

8. Pour the mixture into a blender and process till smooth. Transfer back into the pan and add the lamb. If necessary, adjust the consistency by adding water.

9. Sprinkle the fresh coriander and cook for a further five minutes.

10. Serve hot with brown rice.

Strawberry Phirni

Ingredients

12-15 fresh strawberries

4 tablespoons rice

1 litre milk

¾ cup sugar

½ teaspoon green cardamom powder

8-10 pistachios

6-8 almonds

Method

1. Clean, wash and soak the rice in sufficient water for half an hour. Drain and grind the soaked rice to a coarse paste. Add half a cup of water to the rice paste.

2. Wash, hull and slice two strawberries and finely chop the rest.

3. Soak the pistachios and almonds in hot water for five minutes; drain, peel and slice finely.

4. Heat the milk and bring to a boil. Gradually stir in the rice paste, lower the heat and simmer for three to four minutes, stirring continuously or until the milk thickens.

5. Add the sugar, cardamom powder and continue to simmer till the sugar dissolves. Remove from heat, cool to room temperature and stir in the chopped strawberries.

6. Pour the mixture into earthenware or ceramic bowls, garnish with sliced pistachios, almonds and chopped strawberries and serve chilled.

Shahi Tukre

Ingredients

6 slices white bread

2 tablespoons olive oil

2 cups milk

4 tablespoons sugar

3-4 saffron threads, crushed

1 cup crumbled *khoya/mawa*

½ teaspoon green cardamom powder

15 cashew nuts, chopped

1 tablespoon cudpah nuts

A few drops of rose essence

8-10 almonds, chopped

A few rose petals

1 sheet of edible silver foil

Method

1. Preheat the oven to 180°C/350°F/ Gas Mark 4.
2. Remove the crust from the bread slices and cut each slice into two.
3. Brush olive oil on the bread and bake in the preheated oven for twenty minutes till golden and crisp.

4. Meanwhile, heat the milk with the sugar and saffron. Simmer for twelve to fifteen minutes, or till reduced to three-fourth its original volume.

5. Add the crumbled *khoya*, cardamom powder, half the cashew nuts and half the cudpah nuts. Remove from heat and set aside to cool. Stir in the rose essence.

6. Arrange the toasted bread slices in a baking dish. Spoon thickened milk onto them.

7. Sprinkle the almonds, remaining cashew nuts and cudpah nuts and bake for another fifteen minutes.

8. Decorate with the rose petals and edible silver foil and

9. Serve warm or cold.

Aamras With Kesar

Ingredients

1 kg ripe mangoes

¼ teaspoon saffron threads, roasted and crushed

1 cup sugar, powdered

2½ cups milk, chilled

Method

1. Remove the pulp from the mangoes. Pass through a thin piece of muslin.
2. Add the powdered sugar and the chilled milk.
3. Stir in the saffron. Serve chilled.

Zuccotto

Ingredients

14 slices (200 grams) chocolate sponge cake

1 cup orange juice

1 ¼ cups thick cream

½ cup grated dark chocolate

¼ cup grated white chocolate

⅓ cup almonds, toasted and chopped

⅓ cup hazelnuts, toasted and chopped

⅓ cup glacé cherries, chopped

Method

1. Cut each slice of chocolate sponge into two pieces lengthways. Soak the sponge fingers in orange juice. Line the base and sides of a bowl with the sponge fingers, reserving a few for the top.

2. Beat the cream till stiff. Fold in the dark chocolate, white chocolate, almonds, hazelnuts and cherries and mix well.

3. Pour the mixture into the sponge-lined bowl and cover the top with the remaining sponge fingers. Place in a refrigerator to set, unmould and serve chilled.

GLOSSARY

English	Hindi
Apple	Saeb
Asafoetida	Hing
Babycorn	Chhote bhutte
Basil, fresh	Tulsi ki pattiyan
Bay leaves	Tez patta
Bean sprouts	Ankurit moong
Breadcrumbs	Bread ka choora
Brinjal, baby	Chhota baingan
Brinjals	Baingan
Broad beans	Sem/bakla
Butter	Makkhan
Cabbage	Pattagobhi
Capsicum, green	Hari Shimla mirch
Capsicum, yellow	Pili Shimla mirch
Caraway	Shahi jeera
Cardamoms, black	Badi elaichi
Cardamoms, green	Chhoti elaichi

English	Hindi
Carrot	Gajar
Cashew nuts	Kaju
Cauliflower	Phoolgobhi
Celery	Ajmud
Chicken	Murgh
Chicken, boneless	Haddi rahit murgh
Chickpeas	Kabuli chana
Chillies, dried red	Sookhi lal mirch
Chillies, fresh red	Taazi lal mirch
Chillies, green	Hari mirch
Cinnamon	Dalchini
Cloves	Laung
Coconut	Nariyal
Coriander seeds	Dhania
Coriander, fresh	Hara dhania
Cottage cheese	Paneer
Cucumber	Kakdi/Kheera

English	Hindi
Cudpah nuts	Chironji
Cumin seeds	Jeera
Curry leaves	Kadhi patta
Edible silver foil	Chandi ki varq
Egg	Anda
Fennel seeds	Saunf
Fenugreek, fresh	Methi
French beans	Farasi
Gamboge	Kokum
Garlic	Lehsun
Ginger, dried	Sonth
Ginger, fresh	Adrak
Goat	Bakri
Gram flour	Besan
Green Peas	Matar
Jaggery	Gur
Lemon	Nimbu

English	Hindi
Lentils, red split	Masoor dal
Lettuce leaves	Salad ke patte
Mace	Javitri
Mango	Aam
Mango, unripe, dried and powdered	Amchur
Mint	Pudina
Mushroom	Khumb
Mustard seeds	Rai
Mutton	Gosht
Mutton, minced	Keema
Nutmeg	Jaiphal
Olives	Jaitun
Papaya	Papita
Parsley	Ajmoda
Peanuts	Moongphali
Peppercorns, black	Kali mirch

English	Hindi
Peppercorns, white	Safed mirch
Pigeon peas, split	Toovar dal/arhar dal
Pineapple	Ananas
Poppy seeds	Khuskhus
Prawns	Jheenga
Pumpkin	Kumbda
Refined flour	Maida
Rice, parboiled	Ukda chawal
Rose	Gulab
Saffron	Kesar
Screw pine	Kewra
Sesame seeds	Til
Shallots	Chhote pyaaz
Shrimps	Chhote jheenga
Soda bicarbonate	Khane ka soda
Spinach	Palak
Spring onion	Hara pyaaz

English	Hindi
Spring onion greens	Hare pyaaz ki pattiyan
Star anise	Chakri phool/ badiyan
Sweetcorn kernels	Makai ke dane
Tamarind	Imli
Tomato purée	Pise hue tamatar
Tomatoes	Tamatar
Tomatoes, cherry	Chote tamatar
Turmeric powder	Haldi
Vinegar	Sirka
Wholewheat flour	Atta
Yogurt	Dahi